The Huguenots

or

The Early French in New Jersey

ALBERT F. KOEHLER

CLEARFIELD

Originally published
1955

Reprinted for
Clearfield Company by
Genealogical Publishing Co.
Baltimore, Maryland
1992, 1993, 1996, 1999, 2003, 2007

ISBN-13: 978-0-8063-4637-3
ISBN-10: 0-8063-4637-X

Made in the United States of America

THE HUGUENOTS OR EARLY FRENCH
IN NEW JERSEY

In 1534 Jacques Cartier commanded a fleet fitted out in France under the direction of Francis, King of France, and landed at Newfoundland. Finding himself in a broad river he called it the St. Lawrence, because it was discovered on the feast day of the saint bearing that name. On the river he made the first attempt of the French to form a settlement in America. This and following attempts at colonization failed until 1608, when Champlain laid the foundation of Quebec.

It was through the influence of Sieur de Monts, to whom was granted the fur monopoly in Canada, that in 1604 the Huguenots were permitted to enjoy freedom in the New World. Twenty years later thirty families, mostly religious refugees, settled in the lower end of Manhattan.

Up to 1629 only exploring parties came to New Jersey, to what is now Bergen and Hudson Counties, but in 1630 Michael Pauw obtained two tracts of land, one called Hoboken Hacking and the other Ahasimus. These were parts of what is now Jersey City. Other settlers began to obtain titles to land, many of them French Huguenots.

The name Huguenot was a designation of the Calvinists of France given about the middle of the Sixteenth Century to the Protestants of France. According to

Henry Estienne, the protestants at Tours assembled at night at the gate of King Hugo, whom the people regarded as a spirit. A monk in a sermon declared that they be called Huguenots as kinsmen of King Hugo who also went out only at night. From 1560 on this name was popularly used.

From 1510, when the Reformation under the leadership of Jacques Lefever started to make progress in France, there were successive persecutions of the protestants. In 1560, twelve hundred Huguenots were hanged at Amboise. Catherine de Medici, who was Regent of France for her son Charles IX, by an edict in 1562 granted Huguenots the right to worship outside of walled towns. Infraction of this edict led to the massacre at Vassey three months later, the beginning of eight wars of religion. On August 24, 1572, the terrible massacre of St. Barotholomew took place, when thousands of Huguenots were slaughtered.

Henry IV of Navarre, first of the Bourbon line of French kings who had been reared a Protestant and Huguenot, sought to unite Europe in a compact for the defense of Christendom. On April 13, 1598, he promulgated the Edict of Nantes, giving Huguenots and Catholics equality before the law. He later was converted to Catholicism and was assassinated in 1609.

On October 22, 1685, Louis XIV signed the Revocation of the Edict of Nantes, thus making the exercise of the

Protestant religion unlawful.   There followed one of the most violent persecutions in history, and fleeing from this persecution the Huguenots emigrated by tens of thousands into every country free enough to give them a home.   They carried with them the honor, prosperity and industrial energy of France, and every country which received them they helped to make rich and powerful.   In the discovery of New York and New Jersey the Huguenot was an active participant.   The French Huguenot Abraham Chamberlayne made a large contribution to the funds that enabled Henry Hudson to make his voyage in 1609, when he explored the coast of New Jersey and sailed up the river which bears his name.   Nine years later a trading post was established in the state, though it did not reach the dignity of a settlement.

It was not until 1677 that Huguenot colonists effected a permanent settlement on the banks of the Hackensack, about two miles north of Hackensack and near the "French Burying Ground."   The leader of this colony was David des Marest (de Marest, Demarest), who was born in 1620 at Beauchamp in Picardy, the son of Jean des Marest.   He had been driven by persecution to seek refuge in Holland, where he married Marie Sohier, daughter of Francois Sohier of Niepe, in 1643.   Later he went to Germany and in 1663 came to America, arriving at Nieu Amsterdam on the ship *Bontekoe* (spotted cow) and joined others in the Huguenot colony on Staten Island.

In 1677 David Demarest purchased a tract of land in Tappan District, between the Hudson and Hackensack rivers, afterwards known as "The French Grant." He removed there with his family in 1678, accompanied by Jacques la Rue. Shortly afterwards there were fifteen families, including Nicholas de Voor (De Voe), Jean du Rij (Durie), Andries Tiebout, and Daniel Ribou.

David Demarest is commemorated as the patriarch of this Colony. Forty-seven of his descendants served in the American Revolution, many of them officers.

Jacques Le Roux (Larew, Laroe, La Rue) settled in Hackensack. He married (1) Magdalena Gille and had a son Peter, who was baptized in Kingston, New York in 1688. In 1690 Jacques married (2) Olive, widow of Joshua Cresson of Long Island.

Pierre (Peter) Valleau married Madalene Fauconier, daughter of Peter Fauconier and his wife Madalene, and lived near Paramus, Bergen County. Some of their children were baptized in the Reformed Dutch Church in Hackensack.

Etienne Bourdette, a native of La Rochelle, France, came to New Amsterdam in 1685 and was a member of the French Church, New York as early as 1689. The Bourdettes of Bergen County are descended from this first emigrant.

Nicholas Du Puy and his wife, Catherine Renard De Vos, emigrated from Ar-

8

tois, France in 1662, and arrived at New Amsterdam on the ship *Purmerland Church*. Later they settled in Bergen County, where they joined the Bergen Dutch Reformed Church.

David Provost, the progenitor of the New Jersey family of Provosts, came from Holland to New Amsterdam before April 28, 1639. He was a descendant of William Provost (Prevost) who fled from Paris to Amsterdam, Holland. David Provost died January 1656, in New Amsterdam, leaving a widow, Grietje Gillis, daughter of Gillis Jansen Verbrugge. Their second son David, born in Connecticut, baptized September 3, 1645, bought land in 1698, being at or near Paramus, Bergen County. David, son of David, married Tryntje Laurens of Amsterdam on July 29, 1668, and had eleven children.

Guilliam Bertolf was born at Sluys in Flanders and with his wife Martina Hendricks Verwey came to America in 1684, locating at Bergen County. He died at Hackensack in 1724. He had children: Sarah Demarest, Marie Bogert, Elizabeth Terhune, Henry, Corynus, Jacobus, Martha Bogert and Anna Varrick.

Francois Le Seur (Lozier) was the ancestor of the Lozier family of Bergen County. Francois, born 1625 in Challe Mesnil, three miles south of Dieppe, came to Flatbush, L.I. in 1657. He married 12 July, 1659, in the Dutch Church, New Amsterdam Janatie Hildebrand, daughter of Hildebrand Pieterson. Their son Nicholas married 8 May, 1691, at New York, Trintie, daughter of Peter Slot. They moved to Hackensack and after the death of his first wife he married in January 1709, Antie, daughter of Derick Banta.

The Hasbrouck family of Bergen County is descended from two brothers, Jean and Abraham Hasbrouck, born in Calais, France. In the spring of 1673, Jean and his wife, Anna, (daughter of Christian Deyo, a Huguenot) with their two unmarried daughters, Mary and Hester, came to Kingston, N.Y. It was not until 1675 that Abraham Hasbrouck sailed from Amsterdam to join his brother Jean in Kingston. The records of the Kingston church show under date of 1676 the following marriage entry: "Abraham Hasbrooq of Calais and Maria Deyo of Moeterstat in Duyslant." Abraham died March 7, 1717. His wife died March 27, 1741, in her 88th year. They left children: Jean, Abraham, Isaac, Jacob, Mary--wife of Isaac Du Bois, Hester--wife of Peter Gumaer, Elizabeth--wife of Louis Bevier of Marbletown.

During the religious persecution in France, Jan Baerdan (Berdan) fled to Amsterdam and thence to New Amsterdam, sometime prior to 1682, with his wife and son Jan, Jr. Jan, Jr. went to Hackensack previous to 1693.

Nicholas De Vos (De Voe) of La Rochelle, France went to Manheim in Germany, from where he emigrated to America in 1675. He stopped at New Harlam, where he married Mary See. She died in 1681 and in 1706 he married (2) Margaret Jans.

10

In 1699 he moved to Bergen County and joined the Bergen Church. In 1687 he settled at Hackensack. His children were: Abraham, born 1667; John, born 1669; Hester Brower, born 1671; Susanna Van Gelden, born 1873; Mary Buys, born 1675. Nicholas is buried in the Old French Burying Ground in Bergen County.

The Brower family of Bergen County is descended from Adam Brouwer, who emigrated from Cologne, France in 1642. In 1645 he married Madalena Jacobs Ferdon of Long Island. Some of the grandchildren of the first emigrant moved to Hackensack about 1700.

The Parsell family in Bergen County is of French origin. John Parcil, then a resident of England, emigrated to America with his wife and settled at Dutch Kills, L.I. His grandsons Nicholas and Walter settled in Bergen County.

Jan Tiebout, of French ancestry, was a Court Messenger in Bergen in 1661.

John La Grange, born 1630 in France, was a Huguenot who fled to Holland and thence to America in 1656. His son John died in Bergen County.

Abram De Baun, ancestor of the De Bauns in Bergen and Hudson Counties, descended from Joost de Baen of Flanders, who settled in New Amsterdam in 1683. Joost married Elizabeth Drabb in 1684 and located in Bushwick, L.I., where he was town clerk. In 1686 he removed to New Utrecht and was town clerk there. In

1704 he moved to Bergen County and although his will was dated November 28, 1706, it was not proved until June 4, 1724. He calls himself of "Hackingsack, Essex Co." He had children: Matie--wife of Daniel Samuelse Demarest; Christain--who married Judith Samuelse Demarest; Myke, Carrel, Christina, Jacobus and Marie.

Hendrick Hendricksen Kip, born 1600 in Miewenhuys, married April 20, 1624 to Tryntie Lubberts, came to New Amsterdam in 1637. He was the son of Ruloff De Kype, the Huguenot, the family being settled near Alencon, in Bretagne. Nicholas, a grandson, born about 1666, married Antie Breyant, daughter of Cornelisse Breyant, December 20, 1691, at Bergen, and purchased a large tract of land on the Hackensack River in 1698. He settled at Pollifly, Hackensack and became the founder of the New Jersey branch of the Kip family.

The De Mott brothers, Michael and Matthias, like so many Protestant families who were forced to leave their homes in France, came to America about 1665 and settled in Esopus (now Kingston, New York.). Michael purchased a tract of land between the hills and the Pequannock River in Morris County known as Pompton Plains. This deed was dated October 9, 1704. Michael married Annetje Westbrook in 1682 at Albany and had three sons: John who settled in the English Neighborhood, N.J.; Richard who settled in Raritan, N.J.; and Hendrick, born 1715, who came into possession of the homestead at Pompton Plains.

The Laurence (Lorentz, Laurents) family, protestants, came from La Rochelle, France. They joined the Germans in 1710 in Holland for their departure to America. Johannes Lorentz in New York 1710, gives his age as 43. His will, dated Peapack, New Jersey, July 1745 names his children.

In his "Genealogical History of Hudson and Bergen Counties," C. B. Harvey (1900) gives a long list of the earliest landowners and settlers in Bergen (and now Hudson) Counties. The following French ancestral names, which do not appear elsewhere in this article, are taken from this list. John Alyea from Artois, Balthazer Bayard from Dauphiney, Nicholas Bayard from Alphen, France, William Cornelise from Kalbrist, Claude de la Maistre (Delamater) from Richburg, Mattice Jansen from Cologne, Jan Perie (Perry) from Pont-le-feeks, Petrus Quidore from Havre, Paul Saunier from Mormany, Michael Jan Tibout from Bruges, Symon Fell from Dieppe.

The following were of French lineage but were listed as coming from places other than France: Petrus de Reimer from Amsterdam, Jan Durje from Mannheim, Peter Jay from London, Albert Albertsen Terhune from Hunon, Nicholas Varlet from Amsterdam, Jacques Cortelyou from Utrecht.

From Flanders came the following: Lorens Van Hallen from Limburg, Bartholomew Feurst from Bruges, Cornelius Jansen Marinus from Oostberg, Joost Vanderlynden from Belle, Jacob Jansen Van Etten from Brabant, John Vinge from Bruges, Michael Janson (Vreeland) from Brockhuysen, Peter Winne from Ghent, Flanders.

The second Huguenot settlement in New Jersey was at Princeton. Among the names in the settlement were: Vienney, Tulane, Boissonet, Pothier, Le Goy, Ancellein, Husage, Malon, La Rue, Cheilon and Bona.

Peter Bard, founder of the Baird family, said to have been a native of Dauphiny, was naturalized in this colony in 1713. In 1720 he was appointed a member of Governor Burnett's Council. He died in 1734.

The Bertrand family of Hunterdon County descends from the widow Elizabeth Bertrand of Couhe, Vienne, France, who fled with her children to England and arrived in New Amsterdam in 1693. Probably the name was changed to Bertron.

Francois Gerneaux, a Huguenot from the Isle of Guernsey, came to America and settled near New Rochelle, New York, where he died at the age of 103. The family name was changed after a time to Gano. Francois brought his son Stephen to America as a child. Stephen married Ann Walton and had nine children. One of their sons, Daniel Gano, who married Sara Britton, daughter of Nathaniel Britton of Staten Island, moved to Hopewell, Hunterdon County. Among the children born to them was John Gano, born 22 July 1727.

Elias Corriel, Emanual Corriel and David Corriel, three brothers, came to America from the Island of Corsica. Emanuel settled near Lambertville, N.J.

Abraham Le Roux (Larew, Laroe, La Rue), the emigrant, left France for Manheim and sailed for America about 1680. He was in Kingston on the Hudson in 1688 and 1692. Later he moved to the Huguenot colony on Staten Island. However, he died in Hunterdon County in 1712. Abraham was the progenitor of the New Jersey family.

Andrew Freneau, a native of La Rochelle, France, emigrated to America about 1702. He was for years the agent of the Royal West India Company of France. His grandson Philip Freneau graduated from Princeton in 1771, served in the American Revolution and suffered the horrors of New York prison ships. He was well known as a poet and as editor of the *National Gazette.*

Henri Marchand, born in the vicinity of Caen, France, with his wife and oldest son Henri and other children, came to America about 1685, settling first in Newtown, L.I. Henri, Jr., growing up in Newtown, learned the art of weaving. Before 1698 he had married Ann ---. His will, dated Maidenhead, Hunterdon County, July 1738, names his wife Ann and the following children: Henri, Andrew, Peter, Thomas, Mary, Ann, Rebecca, Elizabeth and Sarah.

By 1686, and even earlier, French Huguenot family names appeared in towns on the Monmouth shore. They were Pierre le Conte, Joseph Roy, John de la Valle, Hance, de la Fontaine, Steele, la Fevre and others. Estelville, N.J., derived its name from the D'Estail family, who settled there in 1671. The families of West Jersey joined with St. Mary's Church in Burlington or the Society of Friends. Large landowners, they brought with them new refinements and gave to their children a love for the beautiful.

Anthony Pintard is named in the Court Records of Monmouth County in 1691 as a merchant. In 1698 he was Assessor of Shrewsbury, a member of the New Jersey Provincial Council in 1701 and Justice 1701-1704. He died in Shrewsbury in 1732. His will, proved May 11, 1732, names his children: Anthony, Margaret, Samuel, John, Lewis, Magdalena Hutchins, Catherine--wife of John Searles, Florinda, Isabella--wife of Isaac Van Dam. He left thirty pounds to the French Church of New York.

Peter Le Conte, a physician of Shrewsbury, owned 500 acres of land near Barnegat in 1734. He married Valerie Eaton, daughter of John. His tombstone near Matawan says he died in 1768, aged 66 years. Dr. Wickes, in his "History of Medical Men of New Jersey," says he was descended from William Le Conte, who came from Normandy after the Edict of Nantes in 1685.   He had three children: William, Dr. Peter and Esther.

Lewis (or Louis) Carree, executor of Anthony Pintard's will, had a son Lewis, who settled for a brief period at Allentown, Monmouth County.   His will was dated there in November, 1732, but he was not named among the taxpayers there in the preceding year.   He named his wife Margaret and son Lewis as executors.   He also mentioned his father (Lewis Carree), John Lewis Pintard and friend Isaac Steele.

Some of the Monmouth County descendants of Garret Vanderveer and his brother David, as well as descendants of Peter Covenhoven (Conover), George Conover and Peter Van Dorn, are descended from The Rev. Benjamin DuBois who was a great grandson of Louis DuBois the Huguenot. Garret A. Hobart (1844-1899), Vice President of the United States from 1896 to 1899, was a descendant of The Reverend Benjamin DuBois.

Pontus (Poncet, Pounsett) Steele came from the little village of Lorieres, near Limoges, France and settled in Staten Island in 1680.   He went to New York and thence to Monmouth County, where in 1692 he was licensed to keep an inn.   His son Gabriel, who bought land near Manasquan in 1714, was a Judge of the Quorum and prominent in public life.   In 1728 Gabriel had a patent for a ferry boat from South Amboy to Staten Island.   He settled in Perth Amboy in 1729.   His children were: Benjamin 1683-1759, Gab-

17

riel 1685-1738, Ambrose 1687 ---, John
1689 ---, Isaac 1690 ---, Eugene 1692
---.

Jacob Trieux (Trewax, Truax) bought
land in Monmouth County in 1676. He was
born in New Amsterdam 7 December 1645.
It is supposed that Jacob was of the
family of Philip du Trieux, court messenger, who settled in New Amsterdam in
1623. A son Isaac went up the Hudson
toward Schenectady.

The Allaire family of Monmouth County descends from the French Huguenot
ancestor Alexander Allaire, son of
Pierre, who came from Rochelle, France in
1699 and settled in West Chester County,
N.Y.

The ancestor of the Rulon family of
New Jersey was Ruel Rulon, a Huguenot,
who settled in Monmouth County. Although
his brothers were Catholics, they helped
him to escape in a hogshead which was
rolled on shipboard and thus he left
France. It is presumed that he landed in
New York. He is mentioned in Monmouth
County records in 1704.

Elias Mestayer of Shrewsbury died in
1731. His will made a bequest to the
poor of the French Protestant Church in
Spitalfields, London, and named Peter Le
Conte, practitioner of physick, as one of
his executors.

Robert Le Cock had land in Shrewsbury in 1679.

Edmund Lafetra, who was among the original settlers of Monmouth in 1667, married a widow named Frances West. Edmund died September 1687, leaving a widow, son Edmund and daughter Elizabeth, wife of John West.

Francois Le Maistre was an original settler in Monmouth in 1667. Later the name was corrupted to Masters.

Mindart Lafever is given in Freehold records as of New York in 1715. The same year he was of Middletown, New Jersey.

Elias De Hart was a constable in Shrewsbury in 1720, a grandson of the Huguenot Simon Aertsen De Hart, who came to America in 1664.

Randall Huet, an original settler of Monmouth in 1669, had previously lived in New Amsterdam.

Alexander Hamilton, son of a Scotch merchant, was born on the Island of Nevis in 1757. His mother was of a Huguenot family, the Fancettes. She died a few years after her marriage, leaving her son Alexander. At the age of 15, Alexander Hamilton left his native island of St. Christopher to come to America. Finding his way to Elizabethtown, New Jersey he was received into the home of Elias Boudinot and started his schooling there.

Jan Barbarie, a Huguenot refugee who was born in France, first settled in New Rochelle, New York. In 1702 he petitioned the Proprietors for a house-lot in

Perth Amboy. His grandson John was collector of customs for the Port at Perth Amboy, 1743-1749. His will, proved September 22, 1770, names his wife Margaret and nine children.

The year 1681 marked the beginning of a settlement in the Raritan Valley, Somerset County, in what is now Bound Brook. Many of these settlers were French Huguenots.

The Berrien family in America descends from Cornelis Jansen Berrien, who was born in Bretagne, France. He came to America 1669, and settled in Flatbush, L.I. His wife was Janet Stryker. He died in 1689 at Newtown, L.I. Peter, son of Cornelius, born in 1672, in 1706 married Elizabeth, daughter of Samuel Edsall. Some of Peter's children moved to Rocky Hill, Somerset County.

Bourgon Broucard, born 1645 in La Rochelle, France, was a Huguenot. In 1665 he married Catherine Le Fevre at Bedford, L.I. Bourgon and his wife were among the earliest founders of the French Protestant Church of New York. They also became members of the Bedford Church. In 1688 he sold his farm and moved to Dutch Kills, L.I. His son Isaac remained on Long Island and took the name of Bragaw, while his other four sons moved to Somerset County about 1700. They were: John born 1678, Jacob born 1680, Peter born 1682, Abraham born 1684.

Joost Durie (Duryea), a French Huguenot, fled with his parents from Picardy, France to Manheim and came to America about 1675. He was accompanied by his wife Magdalena de Fevre and his mother. He settled first in New Utrecht, where he bought a farm which he sold in 1681 to Garret Cornellise (Van Duyn) for 300 guilders and a new wagon. Leaving New Utrecht, he settled near Bushwick, L.I., where he died in 1727. His grandson, Joost, who married Antje Terhune in 1730, settled in Six Mile Run, Somerset County.

Peter Du Mont, who settled in Somerset County about 1699, was a son of Wallarand Du Mont, a Huguenot who lived near Lille, France. He fled to Amsterdam, Holland before coming to New Amsterdam in 1657. In 1664 Wallarand Dumont married Margriet Hendricks, widow of Jan Arentsen. Wallarand died in 1713, leaving sons: Walran, Jan Baptist and Peter, the settler in Somerset County. Peter Dumont's will was proved July 17, 1774, and in it he mentions the following children: John, Hendrick, John Baptist, Peter, Rynear, Abraham, Cattelintje--wife of Christian La Grange, Margaret--wife of George Bergen, Gerrette and Jannetie.

The Gaston family was originally from Foix, Southern France. The earliest certain ancestor of the New Jersey Gastons was John Gaston, a Huguenot, born about 1600 in France. The family fled to Scotland where John married and among other children had three sons, John, William and Alexander, who later emigrated to County Antrim, Ireland about 1660-1680. Joseph Gaston, son of John of Ireland, was born about 1700 in Ireland

and came to New Jersey with his brothers Hugh, John and Alexander. It is presumed that their arrival was through the port of Perth Amboy about 1720. Joseph Gaston lived in Bernards Twp., Somerset County, where he died in 1777, leaving his wife, Margaret. The widow, Margaret, moved to Hardwick Twp., Sussex County with her son Joseph, where she died on August 31, 1795, aged 90 years.

Frantz Lucas of La Rochelle, France came to New York with Johannes Laurents in 1710. He is found at New Rochelle, New York the same year with five children. His son Francis was a witness to a baptism in Somerville in 1719.

Vincent Rougnion (Runyon) was born in Poitou, France about 1643 and came to Elizabethtown Plantations soon after his arrival in 1665. Records show that he married Ann Boutcher in Elizabethtown on July 17, 1668. By 1677 he was in Piscataway, as at that time he had 154 1/2 acres of land allotted to him on the Raritan River. He died in November 1713, his wife Martha surviving him. The will of his son Vincent, dated February 1723/4 and proved March 18 of the same year, names his wife Mary and nine children. Vincent Runyon, Jr. was called "yoeman" of Piscataway.

The Bodines of New Jersey (Middlesex, Essex and Hunterdon Counties) have their origin in the family of le Boudin or de Boudain of Cambray, France. Jean Bodine, a Huguenot, of the Cambray family is said to have removed to the Province

22

of Saintonge, France, where his son was born. He probably settled both in Holland and England before coming to New York, where he settled before November 3, 1677. He settled on Staten Island before 1686 and died there in 1694.

Jean Bodine, son of Jean, was born in France May 9, 1645, and died in New Jersey sometime after March 1736. In May 1701, Jean Bodine purchased 87 acres of land in East Jersey, opposite Staten Island. He married (1) on January 11, 1680, Maria, daughter of Jean Crocheron, one of the emigrants to Staten Island. He married (2) Esther, daughter of Francois and Jeanne Susanne Bridon. There were five children by each marriage.

In 1711 Joseph Roy, of the parish of St. Aubin in the Island of Jersey, came to Boston with his wife and son John. He remained in Boston for eleven years and then removed to Woodbridge, New Jersey. His family finally settled in Basking Ridge, where five generations have lived. The family had originally fled from France to the Island of Jersey.

Robert Vaquellin, a native of Caen, Lower Normandy, France and his wife came to America in 1665 with Philip Carteret on the ship *Philip*. In East Jersey records, Robert is styled Sieur des Prairies (de la Prarie) of Caen, France, whence he gained the name Laprairie. However, from 1675 to 1681 he also used the signature Ro Vauquellin. In 1678 he moved to Woodbridge, where he had obtained a patent for 175 acres of land in 1669. Later he received warrants for 900 additional acres. His wife, Jeanne of Woodbridge, was named sole heiress of his estate. An inventory was made of his estate October 10, 1698.

Thomas Bartow, a son of The Rev. John Bartow, was a merchant at Perth Amboy and held many public offices in the province. He was born after 1705 and was the grandson of General Bertaut, a French Protestant who fled France for England in 1685.

Henry Jacques, a carpenter, who was born in 1620, first settled in Newbury, Massachusetts and became a freeman in 1669. He was married to Anna Knight at Newbury and died in 1687. The name of his son Henry appears on a deed with others in 1667 for settling two townships, including the "Towne now called Woodbridge." Henry Jr. was born July 30, 1649, married Hannah (probably the daughter of John Freeman), and settled in Woodbridge in 1665, where he and his father received a patent of 368 acres from the Proprietors. He died in 1679. His children were: Henry who died in 1750; John who was born in 1674; Hannah who was born in 1675 and Jonathan who was born in 1679.

Reune Piatt, a native of Dauphiny, France, fled to Holland and later came to America, settling at Piscataway before 1680. The New Jersey Archives state that in early deeds he is designated as "Reune Piatt, alias La Flower." Letters of administration of October 16, 1705, gran-

24

ted to his widow Elizabeth give his name as Reyneer (Regnier) Peatt, alias "Le Flure" of Piscataway. His son John was of Somerset County.

Jacques Cossart (Cousart), probably from Bretagne, France, came to America with his family in 1663. A grandson, Jacob, born in 1701 at Brooklyn, died in Bound Brook in 1772. Some of Jacob's children lived in Morris County.

The Rev. Frederick de la Cour (Delliker) was of a French family and held a pastorate in Hunterdon County from 1768 to 1782. In 1786 he married (2) Maria Magdalena Juvenal, daughter of David Juvenal, a Huguenot of Philadelphia. Some of his descendants lived in Morris County.

Eves Bellangee (Bellinger, Ballinger) came from the province of Poitou, France, emigrating first to England and thence to America between the years 1682-1690. In the early work of French heraldry the name is written "de Bellinger."

Ives Bellangee, a weaver, and Christain de la Plaine, who was the daughter of Nicholas de la Plaine and his wife Rachel Cresson, both French Huguenots of New York, were married at Friend's Meeting in Philadelphia in 1697. The minutes of the Meeting state that Ives produced a certificate from Virginia. Ives Bellangee and his wife owned land in Salem County on Oldman's Creek in 1701, later selling it and settling in Little Egg Harbor, Burlington County. Ives died there in 1720, leaving his wife and the following children: Ives, James, Elizabeth, Michael, Susannah, Joshua, Isaac and an expected child.

Shourds states that James Bellangee in 1696 appears to have been a Friend residing in Burlington, where he held some town lots. There was also Henry Bellangee, who in 1684 located 262 acres of land in Evesham Twp., Burlington County. The general opinion is that Henry, James and Ives Bellange were brothers. There is reason to believe that all families in West Jersey named Bellanger or Ballenger are descendants of those above named. The name of Evi (Ives) appearing in many of the families of this section denotes intermarriage with the Ives Bellangee family.

Isaac de Coux (De Cou) was of Huguenot descent. He and his second wife Rebecca emigrated from Arvert, France, and arrived at New Castle on the Delaware in 1686. He died shortly after his arrival and was buried at Chester. Isaac and his first wife, Susannah Ashton, had Jacob, John, Isaac, Elizabeth and Emanuel. Isaac Jr. and Jacob settled in Burlington County prior to 1690.

The historians George De Cou and the Rev. A. Stapleton state that the members of the Huling (Heuling) family were French Protestants who fled France to escape persecution. William and Abraham Huling, sons of Walter and Judith Huling of Gloucestershire, England, came to Burlington County in 1674. Both brothers were members of the Burlington Monthly Meeting of Friends in Burlington and were married with permission of the Meeting. William in 1680 married Dorothy Eves, daughter of Thomas of Burlington, while Abraham married Esther English of Pennsylvania in 1686.

Richard Bessonnett, a native of Dauphiny, settled in Burlington County as early as 1692.

The Gaskills and the Gaskins of Monmouth and Burlington Counties are of Huguenot origin, descending from Edward Gascoyne, a shipwright who had a grant of land in Salem, Massachusetts in 1639. His son Samuel married Provided Southwick. About the time of his marriage the name of Gascoyne was changed to Gaskill and Gaskin. Edward Gaskill with Josiah Southwick bought a mill at Mt. Holly by deed dated March 14, 1701. Edward was located in Burlington County by 1688, when his name is given in a deed as Edward Gascoyne. In the census records of Northampton Township, Burlington County, Edward Gaskill's age is given as 46 in 1709. The age of his wife Hannah is given as 33. Their children were: Joseph, age 14; Zorobul, age 11; Provided, age 9; Samuel, age 6; Edward, age 3. Also listed in the same census are: Josiah Gaskill, age 30 and his wife Rebecca, age 23. Their children are Mary, age 3 and Jacob, age 1.

The name of Du Bois was used as an ancient family surname, both in Artois and Normandy before William the First,

King of England, left his native shore.
Louis Du Bois, son of Christain, was born
in Wicres, near Lille, in northern France
on October 27, 1626. He fled to Holland
to escape persecution and later went to
Manheim, Germany, where he married Catherine Blanchon, a daughter of Matthew
Blanchon, a Huguenot, on October 10,
1655. Two sons were born to them, Abra-
ham and Isaac, before their emigration to
America in 1660. They located first near
Kingston, New York, later at New Paltz.
Nine other children were born to Louis
and Catherine. Abraham married Margaret
Deyo, Isaac married Marie Hasbrouck,
Jacob married (1) Lysebeth Varnoye, (2)
Gerritje Gerritsen Van Nieukirk, Sarah
married Joost Jansen, David married Cor-
nelis Vernooy, Solomon married Tryntje
Gerritsen Fochen, Rebecca died young,
Rachel died young, Louis married Rachel
Hasbrouck, Matthew married Sarah Matty-
sen.

Barent and Louis Du Bois, grandsons
of Louis (sons of Jacob), settled in
Salem County. There are many of their
descendants by the names of Du Bois,
Newkirk, Elwell, Elmer, Shute, Mulford,
Dare, Burroughs, Whitaker, Richman, Ray
still living in Salem County.

The Rev. Benjamin Du Bois was born
March 30, 1739 at Pittsgrove, Salem County. He was the minister of the Reformed
Dutch Churches at Freehold and Marlbor-
ough, Monmouth County, 1764-1827, and a
trustee of Queen's College, now Rutgers
University.

Hypolite Lefevre, French Huguenot, fled his native country and went to England. He was in Fenwick's colony, Salem Tenth, before November 12, 1676, as on that date it is recorded that he was part owner of 6,000 acres in Mannington Twp. He came to Salem Tenth from St. Martin's-in-the-Fields, Middlesex, England. He and his wife Mary had one son, Hypolite, Jr., who married Hannah Carll of Philadelphia. Hypolite, Sr. died in Salem previous to 1698.

The Jaquetts were French Huguenots who emigrated to West Jersey and became large land owners in Penns Neck Twp., Salem County. Paul Jaquett bought land in February 1688/89.

The family of Bassetts came from England in 1621 and settled near Boston, Massachusetts. One of the descendants of William Bassett the Huguenot came from Lynn, Massachusetts in 1691 and settled in Salem, New Jersey, bringing with him his family, including three sons, Zebeddee, Elisha and William. Zebedde went to Delaware, while Elisha, born in Massachusetts in 1682, lived and died in Salem County in 1786, age 104 years. Elisha married Abigail Elizabeth Davis of Long Island. She died in Salem in 1770, age 72 years. Perhaps the Samuel Bassett who bought 150 acres of land near the head of Salem Creek in 1698 was another son of William.

Shourds, in his "History of Fenwick's Colony," says that William Waddington was a French Huguenot and emigrated to this country about 1695. He purchased a large tract of land in Salem County shortly after his arrival. His son Jonathan married about 1728.

The Boudinot family of New Jersey descends from Elias (Elie) Boudinot, son of Jean and Marie (Suire) Boudinot of Marans, France. The family in France had for several generations been identified with the Huguenot cause. Apprehensive of a repetition of the horrors of St. Bartholomew, Elie Boudinot left his native land and went to London. He married (1) Jeanne Barand, who died before he moved to England, leaving five children (all born in France): Pierre, Elias, Abraham, Isaac and Mary. Elie married (2) on November 2, 1686, in London, at the French Church in the Savoy, Susanne Papin, the widow of Benjamin d'Harriette, a distinguished citizen of La Rochelle. The same year they took passage for New Amsterdam. Their children were Magdalene, Susanne, Jean and Benjamin.

Elias Boudinot of Elizabeth, who was the fourth of the family to bear that name, was born in Philadelphia on May 2, 1740. Elias, brother of Elisha, studied law with Richard Stockton and married Hannah Stockton, Richard's sister, on April 21, 1762. Hatfield, in his "History of Elizabeth, New Jersey," says that Elias served on the staff of General Livingston; was appointed Commissary General of Prisoners by Congress in 1777; was appointed to Congress in 1778-1781 and chosen president of Congress in 1782; signed the Treaty of Peace with Great

Britain on April 15, 1783, and in 1795 became Superintendent of the U.S. Mint in Philadelphia. He died October 24, 1821. He was survived by one daughter.

Elisha Boudinot, son of Elias the silversmith of Philadelphia, was born in Philadelphia in 1749. He was a prominent citizen of Newark and served as Associate Judge of New Jersey Supreme Court from 1798 to 1805. The progenitor of the family was Elie Boudinot, the Huguenot emigrant.

Philip Carteret, born 1639, was the son of Helier de Carteret, who was of French descent. At the age of 26, Philip came to America on the ship *Philip* in 1665 from the Isle of Jersey and settled at Elizabethtown. He became the governor of the new territory of Nova-Caesarea or New Jersey. Letters of Administration were granted to his widow Elizabeth on December 30, 1682.

Francoise DuBois, a daughter of Christain and a sister of Louis Du Bois the Huguenot, married Pierre Biljouw (Billiou) in the Walloon Church at Leyden on April 20, 1649. Their daughter Maria baptized in the Walloon Church in 1650, came with the parents on the ship *St. Jan Baptist* on May 9, 1661. In the will of Pierre Billiou, dated September 11, 1699, he mentions his daughter Maria, wife of Arendt Prael (Prall), "who is deceased but left seven children." Marie married Arendt Prall at Wiltwick on June 3, 1670.

Arendt Jansen Prall was born 1647 in Nardy, France. He died in 1725 on Staten Island where he had lived for many years. His daughter Mary Prall married Johannes De Camp, son of Laurens Jansen De Camp, the Huguenot. The De Camp family of Essex County descends from the sons of Johannes De Camp and Mary Prall his wife.

Laurens Jansen De Camp was born about 1645 in Picardy or Normandy and was married in 1676 to Elsie de Mandeville, daughter of Giles de Mandeville, the Huguenot. He came to New Utrecht in 1664 from Holland and was the local pastor of the Staten Island Church in 1719. His son John De Camp was baptized in Flatbush Church on February 2, 1679. About 1701 John married Mary Prall, daughter of Arendt Jansen Prall and his wife Marie Billou. John DeCamp's will was proved in Essex County on May 28, 1766.

Giles Jansen de Mandeville and his wife Elsie Hendricks fled from Rouen to escape persecution and came to America in 1649 on the ship *Faith*, settling first in Nieu Amsterdam. He was born about 1625 in Normandy and was married 1648 in Holland to Elsie Hendricks. He died about 1701 in New Amsterdam. His children married and came to New Jersey, settling in the Passaic Valley. Giles de Mandeville's daughter Elsie married Laurens Jansen De Camp.

The progenitor of the Blanchard family of New Jersey was Jean Blanchard, who married (1) Anna Mahoult about 1686; he married (2) Jeanne Gaulthier in 1695,

32

had one child, Jeanne, born January 20, 1696/7 and baptized in the French Church in New York. On the ensuing October 27, 1697, Jean Blanssard was living at "newcastel en painsiluanie' married (3) Susanne Rezeau in the French Church at New York. His daughter Jeanne married Dirck Dey in 1725. They settled early in life at Lower Preakness, near Paterson. Jean Blanchard died before April 6, 1730. Jean settled in Elizabethtown soon after his third marriage, as he was carrying on a country store at that place as early as 1700. This store was carried on by his son John for many years.

The Farrand family of New Jersey descend from one of the oldest families in France. The patronymical name was Dusson (d'Usson or De Husson). Fleeing persecution, a number of the Ferrands fled, some to England, some to Holland and some to Switzerland. Nathaniel Farrand came to New Amsterdam and later settled in Milford, Connecticut in 1645. His son Nathaniel married Mary Cobb and they had three sons: Nathaniel, Samuel and Daniel. Samuel, born 1681 in Milford, moved to Newark and purchased land there in 1711.

Daniel Perrin, son of Pierre, was of Norman French descent, a Protestant and a Huguenot. He was brought over in the ship *Philip* by Governor Philip Carteret and landed in Nieu Amsterdam July 29, 1665. He took up his abode in Elizabethtown Plantations and in February 1666 married Maria Thorrel of Rouen, France.

Daniel and Maria Perrin had sons Peter, James, Daniel, William. Peter Perrin in 1713 bought a tract of 400 acres of land on the Raritan River, then in Monmouth County. Henry bought 200 acres in Middlesex County. He lived and died there.

Pierre Neau (Noe), a Huguenot, came to Staten Island from England in 1663 on the ship *Bontecoe* (The Spotted Cow). He married Margaret Clark of London in 1659. He first settled on Staten Island and later moved to Elizabethtown, where he was an Associate in 1695. He died in 1709. His son John was a resident of Middlesex County in 1694.

Levi Vincent, born in France in 1676, was one of the Huguenots who fled to England and emigrated to America, settling in Newark Twp., Essex County, where his family resided many years. Levi died in 1763.

Jean Durand, the progenitor of the Durand family of Essex County was a Huguenot refugee from Toulose, France. His name in France was Jean Durand Durapee, this name being discarded when he fled to England, where in 1684 he was naturalized. He came to Derby, Connecticut where he is mentioned in the records in 1685. Whether he studied or practiced medicine in France or England is not known, but he soon became noted in the Connecticut colony as "The Little French Doctor." He left three sons, Samuel, John and Noah.

Pierre Tillou, the ancestor of the Tillou family of Essex County, fled from St. Nazaire, France in 1681, was naturalized in England on March 21, 1682, coming to New York before 1691. A petition dated 1691 asks that Peter Tillou (a French Protestant) with others be made burghers and citizens. A son Vincent Tillou married Elizabeth Vigneau, a daughter of Jean and Elizabeth Vigneau. Vincent Tillou died before September 27, 1709, leaving children--Vincent, John, Ann, Elizabeth, Judith.

The Joline family of Essex County descended from Andrew Joline, who came from Saint Palaise, Saintonge, France about 1686, settling in New York. Baird states that Andre Joline obtained denization in New York on August 6, 1686, and was naturalized April 15, 1893. The will of Andrew Joline, dated June 18, 1741, of Borough of Elizabeth, Essex County, proved the following February 13th, names his wife Mary and the following children: John, Mary--the wife of John Blanchard and their children, Andrew, Ann and Mary (under age).

To Sussex County came Peter Guymard, Jacob (Jacques) Caudebec (Cuddeback) and Abraham de Chambre (Chambers).

Jacques Caudebec was born about 1666 at Caudebec-en-Caux, Normandy. He and Peter Gumaer, both French Huguenots, fled to England or Holland in 1685, thence to Maryland and later to New Amsterdam. In 1690 Jacques married Margarette Provost, daughter of Benjamin and Elsje Aelberts

Provoost. Their son and four sons-in-law were farmers near Shepekunk, along the Delaware in northern New Jersey.

Peter Guymard (Guimar, Gumaer), a French Huguenot, son of Pierre Guimar, was of the Province of Saintonge, France. He accompanied Jacques Caudebec on his flight from France to America in 1685. He married Esther Hasbrouck at Kingston, New York in 1692. Some of his descendants settled hear Shepekunk, along the Delaware in northern New Jersey.

The Garrigues (La Garrigues, de la Garrigues, Garrick) families of New Jersey and Pennsylvania descend from Matthew Garrigues, son of Jean, born 1679 in Languedoc. He fled with his parents to The Hague in 1685. Matthew went to the West Indies and later settled in Philadelphia. He was married May 28, 1702, to Suzanna Rochet (Roche), also a Huguenot. Of their five children, Isaac was born in Philadelphia in 1715 and Jacob, born 1716 in Philadelphia, died in Rockaway, Morris County, New Jersey, and was buried at Morristown. He was the progenitor of the New Jersey (Presbyterian) branch of the family. Matthew died September 6, 1726, age 47 years; and his wife Suzanna died September 30, 1746, age 60 years. Both were buried in the Old Churchyard at 5th and Arch Street, Philadelphia.

The Old French Burying Ground of New Milford, Bergen County, New Jersey marks the site of the French Church of Kinderkamack, which existed about 1682-1696. Tho earliest burial was in 1677 for Mario

36

Sohier, wife of David Des Marest. There
are about 200 persons buried in this
French Community Burying Ground, including nine known Revolutionary War sol-
diers.

"The history of the Protestant Reformation and of the new birth of freedom
in the world---can never be complete
except as it relates the deeds and les-
sons of the French Huguenots."

In preparing this brief history of
the Huguenots and early French in New
Jersey, an attempt was made to record as
many names as possible, but this is not
an exhaustive list. The numerous sources
searched for information revealed many
discrepancies and contradictions, but an
effort was made to check and select ma-
terial from the most authentic sources.

                    Albert F. Koehler
                       Treasurer of
        The Huguenot Society of New Jersey
               26 Berkeley Heights Park
October 1955   Bloomfield, New Jersey

BIBLIOGRAPHY

Huguenot Emigration to America -- C. W. Baird, Vol. I, II

History of Harlem -- Riker

Genealogical History of Hudson and Bergen Counties (N.J.) -- C. B. Harvey

New York Genealogical and Biographical -- Vol. 20, 24, 27

History of New Paltz -- Le Fevre

New Jersey Historical Society Proceedings, Series 4, Vol. 16, 67

New Jersey Historical Society Proceedings, Series 3, Vol. 6

Somerset County Quarterly -- Vol. 1, 5

New Jersey Archives--Wills and Deeds

History of New Jersey -- Raum, Vol. I

History of Essex and Hudson Counties -- Shaw, Vol. I

Passaic Valley -- Whitehead

Fenwick's Colony of New Jersey -- T. Shourds (1876)

Proceedings of the Huguenot Society -- Vol. 5

Register of Ancestors of Huguenot Society of New Jersey -- Taylor (1945)

Memorials to the Huguenots -- Rev. A. Stapleton (1901)

Encyclopedia Britannica

History of Elizabeth -- Hatfield

The Early Germans of New Jersey -- Chambers (1895)

Genealogical and Memorial History of New Jersey -- Lee, Vol. 3, 4

History of Monmouth County -- Lewis Publishing Company, Vol. 2

Cyclopedia of 3rd Congressional District of New Jersey -- Wiley

Moorestown and Her Neighbors -- George De Cou

New Jersey, a Guide to the Present and the Past

Hudson County -- Winfield

The Demarest Family in America -- Mary and W. S. Demarest

Cuddebec Family in America -- Cuddebec (1919)

Daniel Perrin, The Huguenot and His Descendants -- H. D. Perrine

The Provost Family of New Jersey and New York -- Purple (1875)

The Rulon Family -- J. C. Rulon (1870)

My Folks -- L. O. Mershon

History of Hunterdon and Somerset Counties -- Snell

D.A.R. Magazine, October, 1955

Proceedings of the Huguenot Society of Pennsylvania, Vol. XXV

A.F.K.

INDEX

44

DesMarest, David 37
  Marie (Sohier) 37
DeVoe, Nicholas 8,
  10
DeVos, Abraham 11
  Catherine Renard 8
  Hester 11
  John 11
  Margaret (Jans) 10
  Mary 11
  Mary (See) 10
  Nicholas 10
Dey, Dirck 33
  Jeanne (Blanchard)
  33
Deyo, Anna 10
  Christian 10
  Margaret 28
  Maria 10
Drabb, Elizabeth 11
du Rij, Jean 8
DuBoid, Sarah
  (Mattysen) 28
DuBois, Abraham 28
  Barent 28
  Benjamin 17, 28
  Catherine
  (Blanchon) 28
  Christain 28, 31
  Cornelis (Vernooy)
  28
  David 28
  Francoise 31
  Gerritje Gerritsen
  (VanNieukirk) 28
  Isaac 10, 28
  Jacob 28
  Louis 17, 28, 31
  Lysebeth (Varnoye)
  28

DuBois, Margaret
  (Deyo) 28
  Marie (Hasbrouck)
  28
  Mary (Hasbrouck)
  10
  Matthew 28
  Rachel 28
  Rachel (Hasbrouck)
  28
  Rebecca 28
  Sarah 28
  Solomon 28
  Tryntje Gerritsen
  (Fochen) 28
Dumont, Abraham 21
  Cattelintje 21
  Gerrette 21
  Hendrick 21
  Jan Baptist 21
  Jannetie 21
  John 21
  John Baptist 21
  Margaret 21
  Margriet
  (Hendricks) 21
DuMont, Peter 21
Dumont, Reynear 21
DuMont, Wallarand
  21
Dumont, Walran 21
DuPuy, Catherine
  Renard (De Vos) 8
  Nicholas 8
Durand, Jean 34
  John 34
  Noah 34
  Samuel 34
Durapee, Jean
  Durand 34

45

46

50

Waddington,
  Jonathan 30
  William 29
Walton, Ann 14
West, Elizabeth
  (Lafetra) 19

West, John 19
Westbrook, Annetje
  12
Whitaker, --- 28
Winne, Peter 14

www.ingramcontent.com/pod-product-compliance
Lightning Source LLC
Chambersburg PA
CBHW071621290326
41931CB00048B/2936